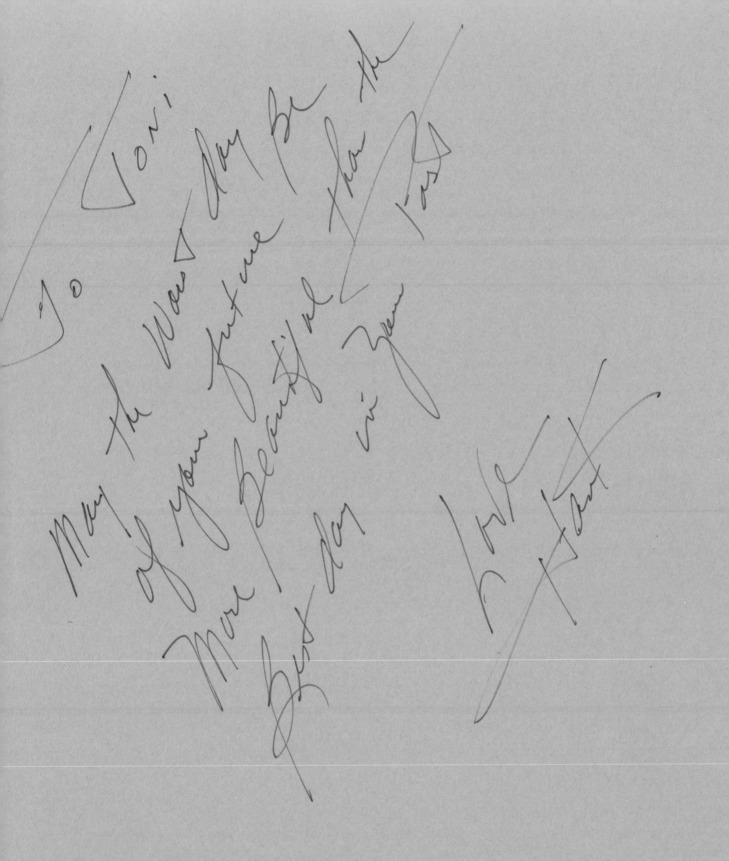

To Toni

May the Worst day of your future be More Beautiful than the Best day in your Past

Love
Grant

Overleaf: Winter storm, Watch Hill

Dedication

When I was a youngster back in the 30's and lived with my parents in New England's northern reaches, "weather" played an important role in our lifestyle. We often huddled around an old oval shaped radio (it would be called an antique nowadays), listening to news reports crackling over the airways. From time to time I recall hearing, "Gale warnings from Eastport to Block Island!" I asked my father, "Where is this place, Block Island, anyway?" He responded with something like, "Oh, it's somewhere out there in the ocean along with Rhode Island." So, for years I thought these remote "islands" were detached places far out in the Atlantic!

Well, it seems there's some validity to this idea anyway. Certainly there are times when Block Island is so isolated by the weather it might as well be out in the middle of the Atlantic. And there were many occasions while doing the photography for this book that I felt as if I were on some distant continent. The "Ocean State" is aptly named. Changing weather, storms, fog and occasional hurricanes sweeping off Long Island Sound and up through Narragansett's narrow channels are the culprits. Activities and lifestyles for the folks living here are influenced and regulated by coastal weather patterns.

It's these natural phenomena that give coastal terrain its identity. But weathered rocks, pounding sea and dancing tides are only a fraction of what the Ocean State has to offer. Diversity, bustling activity and friendly folks are some of the other interesting facets I found in Rhode Island's unique character. I'm pleased to include some of the familiar places and things most folks associate Rhode Island with such as Newport's Mansions, the arrival of the tall ships and scenes around its shoreline communities. But I think you'll agree there are some other surprising aspects as you explore this grand old state through these pages.

I would like to dedicate this book to my wife Elizabeth who accompanied me on all my photographic adventures in Rhode Island.

Clyde H. Smith

Photographs © copyright 1987 Clyde H. Smith
Copyright © 1987 Foremost Publishers, Inc.
This book, or portions thereof, may not be reproduced in any form without the written permission of Foremost Publishers, Inc.
Photographs may not be reproduced in any form without the written permission of Clyde H. Smith
Edited by James B. Patrick
Designed by Donald G. Paulhus
Printed in Japan
ISBN 0-89909-127-X
Published by Foremost Publishers, Inc.
An affiliate of Yankee Publishing Inc.
Dublin, NH 03444

COASTAL
RHODE ISLAND

Photography by Clyde H. Smith
Introduction by Brian Dickinson

Published by Foremost Publishers, Inc.
An Affiliate of Yankee Publishing Inc.

Overleaf: Fishermen aboard the *Maude Platt,* Sakonnet Harbor

Rhode Island's touching of the sea

Rhode Island belongs in body and spirit to the Atlantic, in all weathers. On a breezy day in July, the waters are a playfield; on any gray day of the year, they are a working realm for lobstermen, pilots, quahoggers and tugboat crews. The Atlantic and Rhode Island are one.

On a day of storms, however, the ocean makes its might known beyond any mistaking. In mere hours the wind can rise to gale force, stirring masses of dark water to boil in anger. Wave troughs and crests collide and re-form, their foam tops snatched away by the gale. As a wave line rolls shoreward, its crest climbs steeply as the surge hits the shallows. The storm wave, no longer sustained by its base of deep water, topples over; and in dying, the wave crashes and sends tons of black-green water thundering ashore. Spray leaps skyward, and the land beneath the wave shudders.

Such bouts of fearsome weather are uncommon, but they recall the closeness with the sea that has shaped Rhode Island's past. Centuries before man came to its shores, this corner of North America was kneaded by geological forces, leaving an indented seacoast, several linked-together bays and strings of rounded-off islands. The same ocean that could deliver harsh weather also brought the quahogs, lobsters and menhaden that fed the area's first inhabitants. Rhode Island's ocean arms fostered early commerce among the European settlers, spurred the building of ports and enticed a fledgling U.S. Navy. Up several modest rivers leading to the bays, early settlements spread and prospered. And from the earliest days, the ocean coast offered bracing fresh air and ease, against a seemingly endless panorama of sky and water.

Most of what today is the Rhode Island coastline was formed only a few thousand years ago, when the last great ice sheet, in melting, retreated north and left its imprint as gravel moraines and compressed layers of igneous rock. Under ice as much as a mile thick, the primary rock buckled. As the glacier melted, the sea level rose and encroached on river mouths, giving an initial contour to what later would become Narragansett Bay.

Here and there, as on the peninsula of Bristol or on

Beavertail Point, at the southern extremity of Conanicut Island, hard granite and quartz resisted glacial pressures. To the west, the ice had an easier time. It ground down bumps in the land and, in melting, deposited the boulders and gravel that now form the Rhode Island shore mass between Point Judith and Westerly. This is a flat region, the land scoured by centuries of massive ice and sloping only slowly into the sea. Geologically, this section of coast along southern Rhode Island is known as an outwash plain, representing the final unloading of the glacial burden. The glacier's gift has become Rhode Island's favorite summer playground – a beneficent stretch of broad sandy beaches that runs nearly 25 miles west by south to the boundary of Connecticut.

It is geology that has given Rhode Island its most spectacular natural feature, Narragansett Bay, an arm of the sea that thrusts itself 28 miles northward from the open sea into the state's interior. Although it covers scarcely one-tenth of Rhode Island's total area (some 1,200 square miles), the Bay in many respects is the state's heart. It offers an intimate contact with nature, a source of recreation and an avenue for merchant shipping linking Rhode Island with the world.

The special glory of Narrangansett Bay comes in its islands, large and small. They lend the Bay its character, a fact recognized by Giovanni da Verrazano on his first voyage to those waters in 1524, made on behalf of King Francis I of France. He liked what he saw. There are, he said, ". . . five small islands of greater fertility and beauty, covered with large and lofty trees . . . . In the midst of the entrance there is a rock of freestone, formed by nature, and suitable for the construction of any kind of machine or bulwark for the defense of the harbor."

Verrazano, in an unknowing prediction of the U.S. Navy's interest in the Bay centuries later, told his king, confidently, that "among these islands any fleet, however large, might ride safely."

Rhode Island's embrace by the sea has figured prominently since the arrival in 1636 of a disgruntled divine from the Massachusetts Bay Colony, Roger Williams, who took it on himself to row to Newport from the head of the Bay. As the colony grew, privateers sought to patrol the waters as their own naval force. Pirates and smugglers took advantage of the wandering coastline to ply their trade: a legend holds that Captain Kidd buried treasure on one of the Bay islands. In 1769 patriots burned the British ship *Liberty* and, in 1772, the *Gaspee*, fueling revolutionary fervor. In the Revolution, British ships blockaded the bay and fought lively engagements with the French. In the Nineteenth Century, marine commerce soared, the Bay bustled with vessels of every sort and Newport became the East's most elegant resort. In the Twentieth Century came the Navy and its massive presence at Newport and Quonset Point. For all seasons, to all comers, Rhode Island's coastline had attractions unmatched.

Three elongated islands dominate Narragansett Bay. To the east is Rhode Island (or Aquidneck Island), home of the Navy and of unexampled Newport – Newport with its yachting and tennis; its palatial turn-of-the-century "cottages" built as summer retreats for New York's wealthy; its music festivals and, for a half-century, its America's Cup championship yacht races. All feed Newport's cultivated air of privilege and nautical ambiance. Its Ocean Drive and Cliff Walk, leisurely meanders past rocky coves and imposing mansions, offer world-class ocean vistas.

In Newport Harbor, Rhode Island's land-sea union may shine at its most endearing. On Brenton Cove, tucked into a quiet elbow of the harbor, wavelets lap at a rocky beach. In silhouette, above manicured lawns, lavish rhododendrons frame a few of Newport's grander houses. In the cove, sailboats bob at their moorings and gulls swoop past on their unending quest for lunch.

Eastward lies the Newport waterfront, its trim colonial skyline dominated by the Trinity Church steeple and many newer buildings. To the west stands the granite foundation of Fort Adams and a breakwater that keeps the cove safe in most weather. To the north loom the graceful sea-green towers of the Newport-Jamestown suspension bridge, completed in 1969.

Jamestown itself, due west of Newport, is a homey village

that so far has resisted most pressures of the Twentieth
Century. It lies on Conanicut Island, one-fifth the size of
Aquidneck and dotted with cedar-shingled Victorian summer homes on rambling lawns that reach to the water's edge.
To the north, almost in the center of the Bay, lies the third
largest: Prudence Island, home only to a few clusters of
cottages and a herd of deer.

The state's most famous island, however, is a pork-chop-
shaped hunk of glacial moraine 14 miles out to sea. Block
Island, almost bisected by its "Great Salt Pond" (so named
by Roger Williams), is a rustic summer retreat with idyllic
beaches. Its climate, moderated by the ocean, is normally
10 degrees cooler in summer and 10 degrees warmer in
winter than "America" (as islanders used to refer to the
mainland). The island's protected tracts of shadbush and
bayberry provide a refuge for migrating birds in spring
and fall.

Its waters have also become a graveyard for ships,
including the German emigrant vessel *Palatine,* which ran
aground on Block Island's treacherous North Reef in 1756.
Its crew, having earlier mutinied, abandoned the ship and
left passengers to their fate.

When the colony was new, it was on the rivers feeding the
bay that commerce especially thrived. At the head of the
bay, in Providence, there were boatyards, wharves, cooper-
ages, chandlers and taverns. This was a hub of seagoing
trade, home of families such as that of John Brown,
whose lively shipping interests in the Eighteenth Century
brought in unimagined riches.

On the Blackstone River in Pawtucket, water power per-
mitted Samuel Slater in 1790 to build a mill housing the first
successful Arkwright cotton-spinning machine in the United
States. With it came the start of an industry that would
revamp the economy of all New England. To the east are
small languid streams such as the Barrington and Warren
Rivers. Still farther east, near Fall River, Massachusetts,
rivers such as the Taunton meet in the shallows of Mount
Hope Bay, where currents and winds can be capricious for
sailors.

Rhode Island's southeastern corner, beloved of many but

unknown to most, is a quiet enclave of farms, stone walls and clapboard houses that remain immune to time. This is the domain of Little Compton, a quiet town where rusticity rules. It borders on the Sakonnet River, which is not a river but an arm of the sea. Little intrudes here – there are few crowds and no large-scale commerce – and this suits the residents fine.

Up and down Narragansett Bay, small towns, each one a thriving port, have figured prominently in Rhode Island's evolution. On the bay's eastern flank, proud Bristol was prospering as a commercial center when Newport was in economic ruin after the War of 1812. Today its Poppasquash Point (once called "Pappoosequaw Point") is dotted with elegant waterfront estates.

On the western shore, the village of Pawtuxet (no, not Pawtucket or Pawcatuck, but Pawtuxet) was one of the original "Providence Plantations" (a term that still constitutes a part of the state's legal name). Southward on the western shore, East Greenwich and Wickford bustled as seaports after the Revolution, then sharply declined and only today are showing renewed vitality.

Still farther south, Narragansett Pier was a thriving summer watering place before the turn of the century. By 1880, recalls one historian, it had grown to "a compact mushroom town of inns and hotels of all sizes and varying degrees of discomfort." Now, although nearly all the rambling old hotels have gone, the town still boasts fine beaches and its own imposing avenue of oceanfront homes built with the panache and excess of the Victorian years.

At Point Judith, Rhode Island's coast turns a sharp corner and heads west. The point is said to have been named for Judith Quincy, whose husband, John Hull, was coiner of the famous pine-tree shilling of 1652. By now the summer beach houses are less grand. Here begins a domain of shingled cottages and occasional clam shacks, with dunes held in place by beach grass, beach heather and the beach rose, or *rosa rugosa*. Here, for many, is the only true Rhode Island.

Formally Washington County, it is properly "South County" to nearly everyone, and each of its beaches has a distinctive imprint. From the east, these include the family-oriented (and tame) Wheeler State Beach near Point Judith;

the steeply shelving East Matunuck State Beach (whose sharp undertow once gave the writer a nasty fright); quieter Green Hill Beach, for decades a summer retreat for those who built modest cottages nearby; and Moonstone Beach, which drew notice in the 1970s as being especially hospitable to the unclothed.

Continuing west past the tidal surges of the Charlestown Breachway, a beach-seeker comes upon the state's longest uninterrupted stretch of sand, Quonochontaug Beach, which forms the seaward boundary to the large salt pond of the same name. This becomes the wild and rather remote East Beach before meeting another cove or two and then the endearingly raffish pulse of the resort of Misquamicut, with its clam shacks, water slides and other amusements. Finally, as if flirting with the roiling Long Island Sound waters and the once-formidable claim of Connecticut, Rhode Island's shoreline hooks playfully seaward at the elegant summer retreat of Watch Hill, where fragile and constantly shifting sands have formed the glorified sandbar known as Napatree Point.

Rhode Island's coast is seldom silent. To nature's sounds – waves, gulls, wind – the modern age has added its own. Bell buoys, marking rocks and shoals, give forth with a stately clang as they are jostled by waves. Ships' whistles let everyone within miles know of their passage up or down the Bay. When the mist settles in, foghorns bleat their own warning. On the beaches, young people stroll with outsized portable radios offering pop tunes to the greater world. And back from the water's edge stand the gathering places of summer: beachfront restaurants, clam shacks, bars and amusement parks, all with their juke boxes, electronic pianos or calliopes to spread their exuberance across the summer air.

For all of them – all the sunbathers, hikers, sailors, quahog-rakers, lobstermen, artists and beachcombers – the ocean and its attendant waterways feed the essence of Rhode Island. The Atlantic has made the state what it is: a small but lively enclave of independent-minded folk who relate to the sea and feel its impact. The sea gives Rhode Island much of its special spirit – a spirit conveyed by Clyde Smith's beautiful photographs.

Brian Dickinson

Spring, Brown University, Providence

Colonial door and appropriate motifs, Wickford

Cherry blossoms frame a gazebo

Waiting for the "big one," Beavertail Point, Jamestown

Foggy morning sail, the Newport Bridge

Colorful pastoral, Wakefield

A Newport summer cottage

Overleaf: Rocky promontory, Warren's Point

Preparing for Winter at a seaside farm

Goose Wing Farm, Little Compton

Magnolia pastel, East Greenwich

Union Cemetery on the Commons, Little Compton

Sublime moment, Prescott Farm, Middletown

Feeding the ducks in Wilcox Park, Westerly

Welcome lights, Belcourt Castle, Newport

After five o'clock, Providence

Overleaf: Wickford, North Kingstown

Riverside and Bullock's Cove

Pomham Lighthouse, Riverside

Fishing on the eastern shore

Seaside roses, Hog Island

Tender moments, Prospect Terrace, Providence

Magnolia detail, Apponaug

Overleaf: Brown University, Providence

On the ocean, Narragansett Pier

Seaside garden, Portsmouth

Packing fish for New York's Fulton Fish Market

Mending the fishing nets, Sakonnet Harbor

A cold morning in Jamestown

Barred Owl, Narrow River

Canoeing at dawn on the Pettasquamscutt River

Sunset over the Newport Bridge

Financial district, Providence

First Baptist Church in America, Providence   *Overleaf:* Newport Mansions and famous Cliff Walk

St. George's School, Middletown

Wildflower bouquet, Weekapaug

Forsythia, Spring's first color

Joseph Miranda, stone wall builder

Fresh fruit and beloved Johnny Cake corn meal

Mimi Whitmarsh and fresh baked bread, The Provender, Tiverton

Overlooking Sakonnet Point and Passage

Cormorants at entrance to Old Harbor, Block Island

Overleaf: Newport Harbor and beyond

Tall Ships festival, Newport

Tall Ships and entourage, Newport

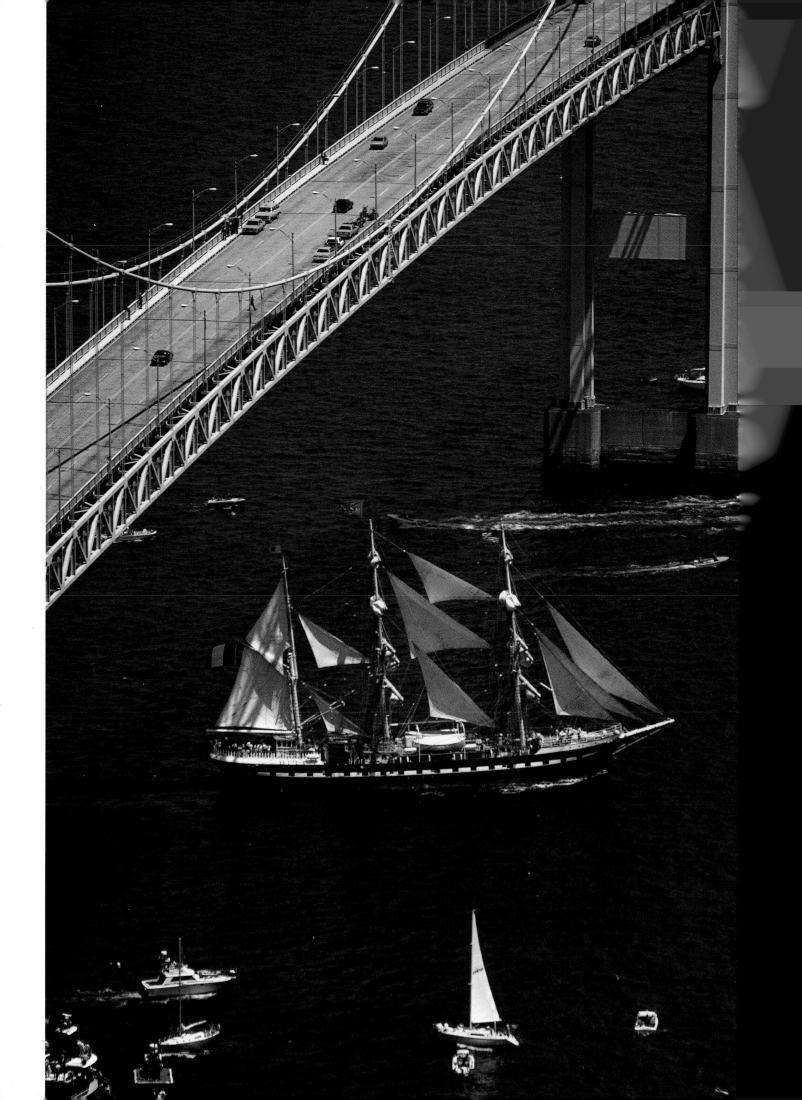

Barrington River, Warren

Along the Barrington River

The 1750 Casey Farm, Saunderstown

Archie MacLaughlin and friend, Saunderstown

Clamming, Nonquit Pond, Tiverton

Watch Hill in the off-season

Overleaf: Block Island

Newport Harbor and its multiple use   Tall Ships, Newport State Pier

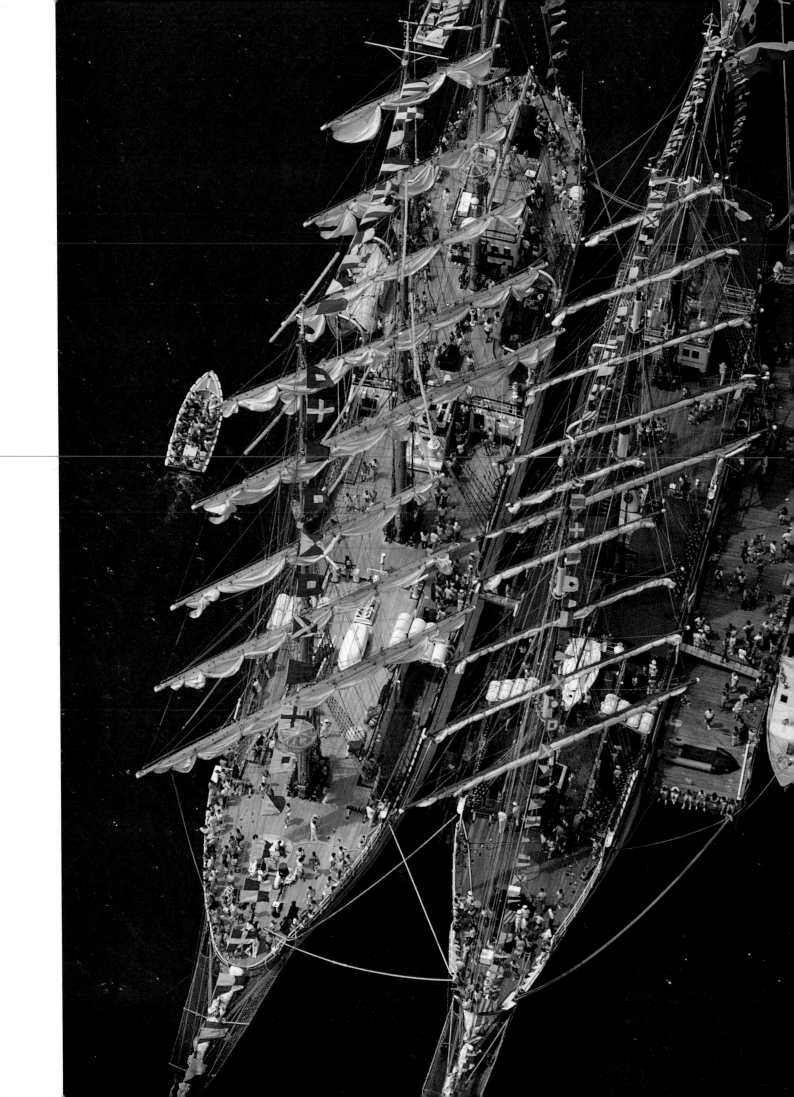

Cassie and Melissa Minto, Watson Farm, Jamestown

Lunch break, Saunderstown

Entrance to Watson Farm, Jamestown   Quiet inlet, Block Island

Colt Mansion, Bristol

Colt Mansion, Bristol

Walker's Farm, Little Compton

Walker's Country Stand, Little Compton

Overleaf: The Bluffs, Block Island

Windmill, Jamestown

Apple blossoms, Warwick

Old clock in The Provender, Tiverton

Winter sojourn, Block Island

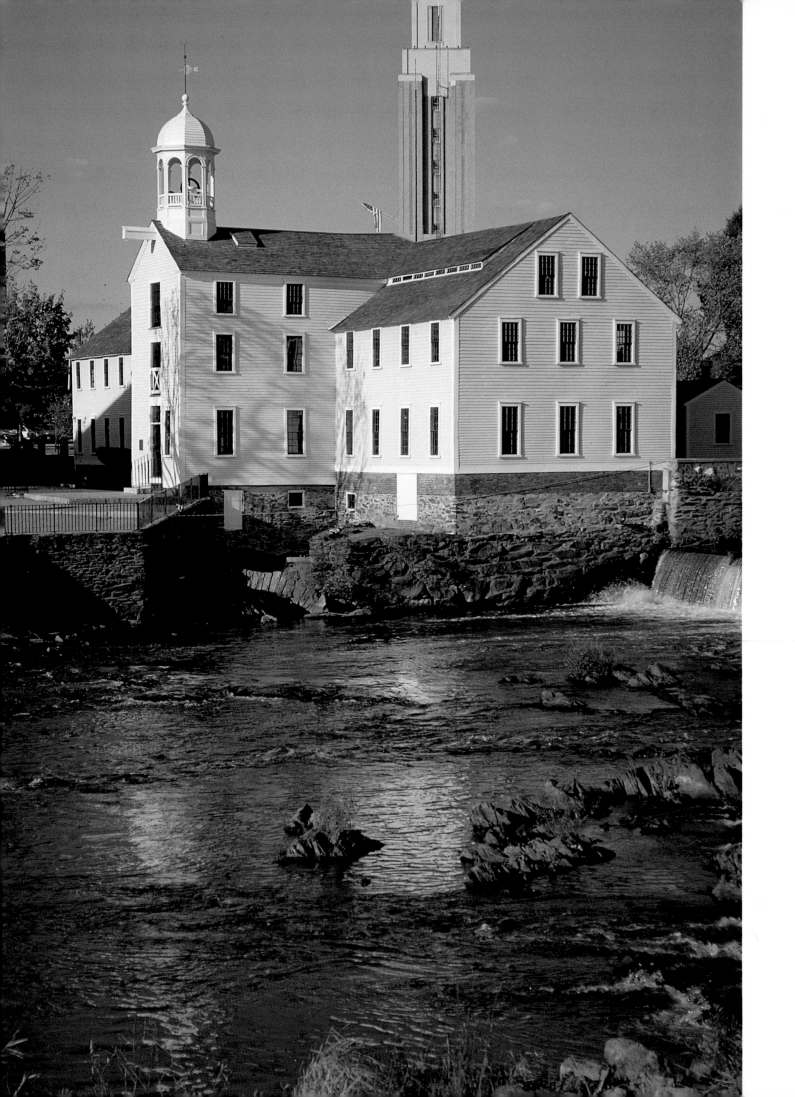

Old Slater Mill, 1793, Pawtucket   Maple leaves at their peak, Cowesett

Cleaning after the day's catch, Sakonnet

Workdays start and end early at Sakonnet Harbor   *Overleaf:* Salve Regina College and Newport Harbor beyond

A mackerel harvest

Fishing Village, Pt. Judith

Beavertail Lighthouse, Jamestown   Swan, Ninigret Pond

Daily chores at Casey Farm, Saunderstown Seaside farm, Quicksand Pond

General Store, Adamsville

Central Baptist Church, Tiverton

Overleaf: Providence from the East Side

Summer cottages in hibernation

Red Tail Hawk, Goddard Memorial State Park

William Vanderbilt's Marble House, Newport

Tall Ships Festival, Newport

Entrance to Great Salt Pond, Block Island

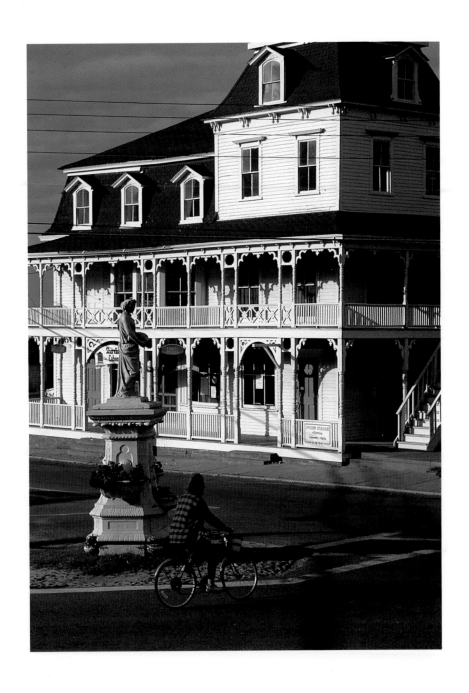

Victorian splendor, Block Island

The State Capitol and Providence

Rhode Island School of Design student, Providence

Overleaf: Southeast Light, Block Island

Pt. Judith Lighthouse

Near the Cliff Walk, Newport

Gambrelled roof farm, Newport

Prescott Farm, Middletown

Tulips, Benefit Street, Providence

Mirrored sunlight, Ninigret

Wakefield